STRANGE *but* TRUE ANIMALS

BY LORI POLYDOROS

Reading Consultant:
Barbara J. Fox
Reading Specialist
North Carolina State University

CAPSTONE PRESS
a capstone imprint

Blazers is published by Capstone Press,
151 Good Counsel Drive, P.O. Box 669, Mankato, Minnesota 56002.
www.capstonepub.com

Books published by Capstone Press are manufactured with paper
containing at least 10 percent post-consumer waste.

Library of Congress Cataloging-in-Publication Data
Polydoros, Lori, 1968–
  Strange but true animals / by Lori Polydoros.
    p. cm. — (Blazers. Strange but True.)
  Includes bibliographical references and index.
  Summary: "Describes unusual animals and their strange behaviors"—Provided by publisher.
  ISBN 978-1-4296-4551-5 (library binding)
  1. Animal behavior—Juvenile literature. 2. Animals—Juvenile literature. I. Title. II. Series.
  QL751.5.P65 2011
  590—dc22   2009050389

Editorial Credits
Editor: Kathryn Clay
Designer: Kyle Grenz
Media Researcher: Svetlana Zhurkin
Production Specialist: Laura Manthe

Photo Credits
Alamy/Danita Delimont, 28–29; Visual&Written SL, 16–17; WaterFrame, 24–25
AP Images/Ifremer, A. Fifis, 22–23
Copyright NORFANZ: Image has been provided courtesy of the NORFANZ partners–National
    Oceans Office, CSIRO, the NZ Ministry of Fisheries & NIWA, 8–9
Corbis/Frans Lanting, 6–7
Dreamstime/Dejan Sarman, 4–5; Omar Ariff Kamarul Ariffin, 14–15
Getty Images/Photolibrary/David Haring, cover
Nature Picture Library/David Shale, 26–27; John Cancalosi, 10–11
Peter Arnold/Wildlife, 12–13
Photolibrary/Morales Morales, 20–21
Photo Researchers/James A. Hancock, 18–19
Shutterstock/Andrejs Pidjass, cover (texture)

TABLE OF CONTENTS

Strange Creatures 4

Naked Mole Rat 6

Blob Fish 8

Horned Lizard 10

Aye-Aye 12

Bird of Paradise 14

Red-Lipped Batfish 16

Almiqui 18

Matamata Turtle 20

Yeti Crab 22

Spanish Dancer 24

Glass Squid 26

Wacky and Wonderful 28

Glossary 30

Read More 31

Internet Sites 31

Index 32

STRANGE CREATURES

Strange creatures live all over the world. Sea slugs dance in the ocean. Blood-squirting lizards roam the desert. Birds shake bright feathers. Their odd ways help these animals stay alive.

NAKED MOLE RAT

Naked mole rats live in large groups underground. They can't see. Instead they use their whiskers like **sensors**. The sensors help them know when enemies are near.

sensor—a body part that sends messages to the brain

whiskers

STRANGE but TRUE

Naked mole rats are related to porcupines, chinchillas, and guinea pigs.

BLOB FISH

This Australian fish looks like a floating bowl of jelly. Blob fish have gooey bodies, big noses, wide lips, and cartoon eyes. They float above the ocean floor.

Female blob fish sit on their eggs like birds.

HORNED LIZARD

Horned lizards look like tiny dragons. When scared, the lizard fills its body with air. It might even squirt blood from its eyes. This action scares away enemies.

Horned lizards can double in size when filled with air.

AYE-AYE

Aye-ayes are found only on the island of Madagascar. These **primates** have huge eyes and pointy claws. They spend their days curled up in nests of leaves and twigs.

primate—any member of the group of intelligent animals that includes humans, apes, and monkeys

STRANGE but TRUE

Aye-ayes tap on trees with their long fingers. They listen for insects under the tree bark.

BIRD of PARADISE

Male birds of paradise shake their long, colorful feathers. Sometimes they hang upside down. Their fancy dances attract female birds.

RED-LIPPED BATFISH

Red-lipped batfish have a small rod on their heads. The rod works like a fishing pole. Small fish, crabs, or shrimp swim near the rod. Batfish gobble them up.

rod

ALMIQUI

Almiquis (ahl-mee-KEEs) look like brown rats with long, spiky hair. Scientists thought almiquis were **extinct**. But one was found in Cuba in 1999.

extinct—no longer living; an extinct animal is one that has died out

STRANGE *but* TRUE

Scientists know very little about almiquis. Only 36 have been caught for study.

MATAMATA
TURTLE

Matamatas are large freshwater turtles. They have long, flat heads and bumpy shells. Matamatas rest in shallow water. They suck in fish that swim by.

YETI CRAB

STRANGE but TRUE

The yeti crab was discovered in 2005.

Yeti crabs live on the ocean floor. The crabs are small and blind. Their arms and legs are coated with white hairs. The hair traps **bacteria**. Some scientists think yetis eat the bacteria.

bacteria—one-celled microscopic living things that exist all around you

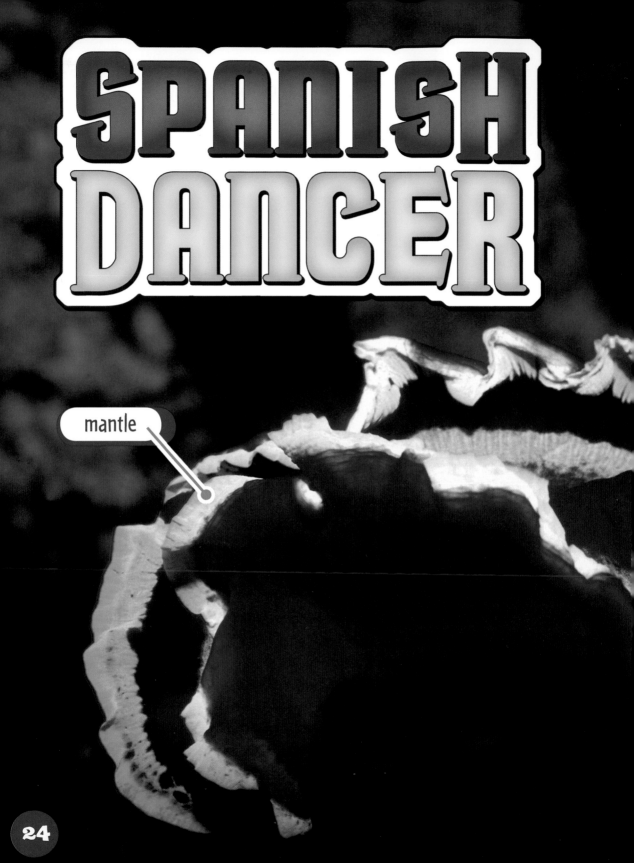

SPANISH DANCER

mantle

These sea slugs can grow up to 16 inches (41 centimeters).

Spanish dancers swim along the floor of warm-water oceans and seas. They unroll the ruffled edges of their **mantel**. This ruffle looks like a dancer's swirling skirt.

mantle—a soft extension of the body

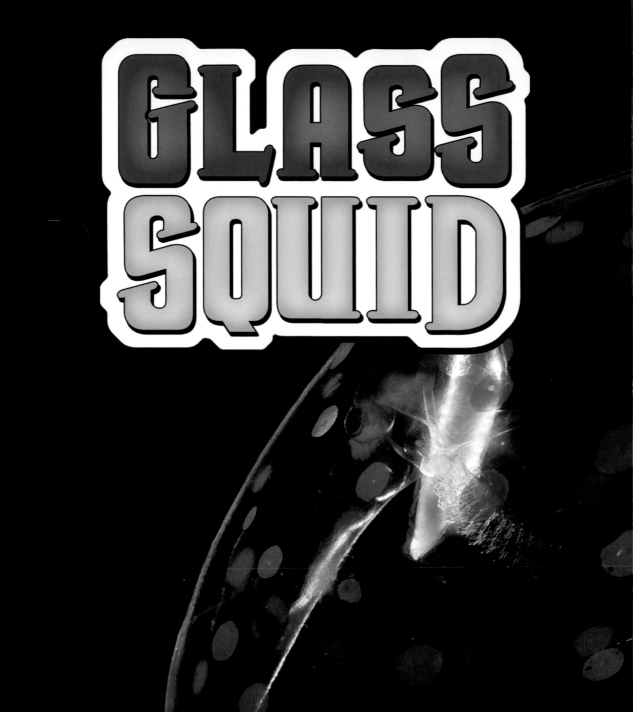

GLASS SQUID

Glass squid float across the ocean like beach balls. When scared, the glass squid puffs up its body with water. It fills with ink and disappears into the dark water.

WACKY *and* WONDERFUL

Animals have surprising skills to help them catch food, find mates, or stay safe. Some creatures may look and act strange. But their wacky ways make them truly amazing.

GLOSSARY

bacteria (bak-TEER-ee-uh)—one-celled, microscopic living things that exist all around you and inside you; some bacteria cause disease

extinct (ik-STINGKT)—no longer living; an extinct animal is one that has died out, with no more of its kind

mantel (MAN-tuhl)—a soft extension of the body

mate (MATE)—the male or female partner of a pair of animals

primate (PRYE-mate)—any member of the group of intelligent animals that includes humans, apes, and monkeys

sensor (SEN-sur)—a body part that sends messages to the brain

READ MORE

Ablow, Gail. *A Horse in the House, and Other Strange but True Animal Stories.* Cambridge, Mass.: Candlewick Press, 2007.

Bredeson, Carmen. *Fainting Goats and Other Weird Mammals.* I Like Weird Animals! Berkeley Heights, N.J.: Enslow Publishers, 2010.

Miller, Connie Colwell. *Disgusting Bugs.* That's Disgusting! Mankato, Minn.: Capstone Press, 2007.

INTERNET SITES

FactHound offers a safe, fun way to find Internet sites related to this book. All of the sites on FactHound have been researched by our staff.

Here's all you do:

Visit *www.facthound.com*

FactHound will fetch the best sites for you!

INDEX

almiquis, 18

aye-ayes, 12, 13

bacteria, 23

birds, 4, 9, 14

birds of paradise, 14

blob fish, 9

Cuba, 18

deserts, 4

eggs, 9

enemies, 6, 10

feathers, 14

glass squid, 27

horned lizards, 10, 11

insects, 13

Madagascar, 12

mantels, 25

matamata turtles, 21

mates, 28

naked mole rats, 6, 7

oceans, 4, 9, 23, 25, 27

primates, 12

red-lipped batfish, 16

Red Sea, 25

sea slugs, 4, 25

sensors, 6

Spanish dancers, 25

yeti crabs, 22, 23